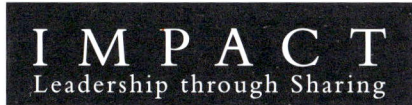

Outsourcing Working Group

Best Practice Guidelines for Outsourcing

Presented by:
KPMG IMPACT Programme
8 Salisbury Square
London EC4Y 8BB
Tel: 0171 311 1000
Fax: 0171 311 3993

London : HMSO

Management Summary

These Guidelines, developed by an IMPACT* Working Group, are aimed at business and IS managers who have decided to outsource part or all of their services and are trying to maximise the benefits that result. The emphasis throughout is on practical guidance for busy executives in managing outsourcing contracts, based on the experiences of over 100 organisations. A detailed breakdown of the Guidelines is given in the Contents on the following page.

© KPMG 1995

Applications for reproduction should
be made to HMSO's Copyright Unit

ISBN 0 11 702012 5

*The KPMG IMPACT Programme is a partnership of major user organisations which have been collaborating since 1989. Each is committed to making the most effect use of IS through learning from each others' experience. The basic principle behind the work of the programme is that the managerial implications of IS are ill understood and the way forward is not through theory but through the study and application of best practice. New members are always welcome.

Foreword

Although organisations have utilised third parties for many years in augmenting the delivery of Information Systems (IS), it has been only recently that significantly larger portions of IS and much more critical functions have been "outsourced" to third parties. This newly expanded market of service providers, with their ever increasing customer base, has resulted in some successful relationships meeting and exceeding expectations. Yet there have not been met, leading to major concerns and issues for all involved.

These Best Practice Guidelines compiled by KPMG IMPACT should be a must reading and a basis of assessment for those organisations considering engaging third parties in providing Information Services. I would even encourage third party providers to read and understand them, as they are a reflection of what has been happening in the marketplace to date. This will ensure a higher degree of success in having both parties define, develop, implement and manage a value-added IS relationship meeting the true needs of the end user. For those organisations that have already implemented a multi-user relationship these Guidelines should still aid in "testing the temperature" of the current relationship and perhaps suggesting areas to further improve it.

Vaughan W Hovey
Manager, IS Supplier & Alliance Management, Eastman Kodak Company

The trend towards the outsourcing of IS Service delivery functions evident in the United States over recent years has now spread to Europe and the UK is its fastest growing market. Research suggests this explosion in outsourcing in Europe will continue beyond the millennium. From this it is clear that IS outsourcing will impact the work of a wide range of business managers and IS professionals.

The decision to outsource, and the basis upon which to construct the outsourcing transaction, is complex. The subsequent task of managing the outsourced relationship is demanding. This compilation of Best Practice Guidelines, derived by the KPMG IMPACT Programme, serves as an invaluable source of reference for any organiationsation facing these challenges.

The approach taken in establishing an outsourcing relationship depends ultimately upon the client's underlying objectives. These may have been set at an operational level, concentrating on cost control and service delivery performance, or they may focus at a more strategic level, where the client is seeking to access the outsourcer's core capabilities in exploiting IS more effectively in support of his business. The Guidelines provide useful best practices and recommendations for those operating at either end of this spectrum.

Guy Griffiths
 IT Director, British Aerospace plc

Contents

Fold-out sheets at the back of the report contains a copy of the Section 2 Checklist.

1 Introduction

1.1 Many Information Systems (IS) functions are being affected by outsourcing, whether it be instigated as a consequence of corporate policy, Compulsory Competitive Tendering (CCT) or Market Testing. Considerable analysis is available on the rationale and contractual aspects of establishing an outsourcing agreement, but much less analysis on how to manage a partially or totally outsourced situation once the contract has been let.

1.2 A poorly managed outsourced situation can have severe financial and service consequences, therefore an IMPACT Working Group has undertaken to identify the best and worst consequences of outsourcing and produce best practice guidelines based on the experiences of over 100 organisations. These Guidelines for outsourcing are aimed at business and IS executives who have decided to outsource part or all of their services and are seeking to maximise the benefits of the outsourced situation.

1.3 As we researched outsourcing experience, it was apparent that many organisations had underestimated the necessary cultural changes and given inadequate consideration to the best means of establishing a challenging and well informed business relationship with the service providers. These Guidelines are designed to help managers learn from a wide range of experiences. It is intended that they should be updated as necessary in the light of further experience

1.4 The report consists of six sections and six appendices. Section 1 contains a brief introduction and Section 2 consists of practical, best practice checklists, the majority of which should be self-explanatory. For the reader who requires a fuller understanding of the rationale for any of the checklist items, a fuller explanation of each is contained in Section 3. Sections 4, 5 and 6 are concerned with key management appointments, understanding and communications between the outsourced customer and supplier. Section 4 contains a summary of the general characteristics of successful Customer and Supplier Contract Managers; Section 5 identifies the important elements of Service Level Agreements (SLAs) necessary to ensure clear definition of service expectations and Section 6 contains a typical review meeting agenda.

1.5   The Guidelines Checklist contained in Section 2 is expected to be the most frequently referenced part of the report. A fold-out copy of the checklist is included at the back of the report to allow ease of reference when reading other sections.

1.6   The appendices provide a range of supporting information including a list of best and worst consequences of outsourcing based on the experience of over 100 organisations (Appendix 3). For the reader who requires further reading Appendix 5 contains a bibliography of over 40 IS outsourcing reports.

1.7   The report concludes with acknowledgement of the many organisations which contributed to the guidelines with particular appreciation to the Working Group members who worked with such enthusiasm in preparing these Guidelines.

1.8   Peculiar circumstances may arise in the situation where outsourcing is the result of a market test which has been won by the in-house team. In these circumstances the organisation is faced with dual roles and the challenge of establishing internal partnerships. The guidelines are considered to be relevant in this situation although they do not specifically address it. IMPACT includes organisations, for example Employment Department, that are addressing this challenge - IMPACT would be pleased to make introductions to organisations in similar situations.

1.9   Comments and suggestions on the Guidelines are encouraged. Please contact Mike Stubbs at the IMPACT office at the address on the title page.

1.10   A benchmark has been developed by IMPACT which provides an assessment of an organisation's relationship with its outsourcing supplier and produces practical recommendations to strengthen the relationship and maximise the benefits. Details may be obtained from the IMPACT office at the address on the title page.

2 Guidelines for the management of Outsource Service Providers – Checklist

Introduction

2.1 This section consists of practical, best practice checklists, the majority of which should be self-explanatory. The checklist items are grouped within headings but are not in any particular order within groupings. For the reader requiring a fuller understanding of the rationale for any of the checklist items, an explanation of each is contained in Section 3.

2.2 The explanations in Section 3 appear in the same sequence as the guidelines in this section. Therefore, for example, the expansion of Guideline 7 in Section 2 is contained in expansion point 7 of Section 3.

2.3 The Guidelines are intended to be concise. They may not be applicable to every situation – refer to the expansion in Section 3.

2.4 The Guidelines Checklist contained in this section is expected to be the most frequently referenced part of the report. A fold-out copy of the checklist is included at the back of this report; it is designed to be opened out and used as a reference when reading other sections.

Definition of Terms

2.5 Four terms are used throughout this report. Their meaning is as follows:

i) 'Customer'

This term is used both to refer to the co-ordinator of the organisation being supplied with outsourced services and to refer to the organisation as a whole. (Other reports may refer to the `customer' as the `client organisation'.)

ii) `End-User'

This term is used to refer to the person, or a representative of the people, in the customer organisation who uses the outsourced service.

iii)`Business Manager'

This term is used to refer to the business sponsors of IS in the customer organisation.

iv)`Supplier'

This term is used to refer to the organisation that provides the outsourced service. The term is used in the singular although, in more complex situations, it is likely to refer to the plural.

Impact Outsourcing Guidelines

Management Issues

1   Retain in-house control over strategic direction.

2   Retain responsibility for setting standards to which the supplier must conform.

3   Use a prime contractor.

4   Make the supplier responsible for delivery.

5   Be prescriptive about the service requirements rather than the method of service delivery.

6   Never lose sight of the business driven objectives of outsourcing.

7   Avoid lock-in to a single supplier.

8   Expect value for money but accept the supplier's need to make a profit – a partnership.

9   Understand the strategic, political and managerial implications of the scope of your outsourcing.

10   Define supplier's points of contact - ensure adherence.

11   Having an appropriate person to manage the contract is key (see Section 4).

12   Keep the procedures simple.

13   Regularly review the outsourcing contract and relationship with the supplier.

14   Never stop negotiating.

15   Re-tender contracts at defined intervals.

16   Regularly review the outsourcing market to identify trends and changes.

17   Monitor supplier's resource levels and business knowledge.

18   Encourage co-operative contract evolution to take advantage of developing technologies.

19   Retain and exercise the right to conduct IS audits at supplier's premises.

20   Aim for continuous improvement.

Human Resource Issues

21   Ensure sufficient number and quality of in-house staff remain to manage the outsourced situation (see Section 4).

22   Promote a continuing bond between supplier staff and end-users.

23   Make the morale of supplier staff a customer concern.

24   Sort out personality conflicts as soon as possible.

25   Review regularly in-house staff skills and numbers.

26   Involve end-users in monitoring service delivery against targets (see Section 6).

27   Retain the right to veto supplier's choice of key staff.

Service/Business Issues

28   Match expectations with needs, not historical achievements.

29   Have a contingency escape plan covering the outsourcing contract, software ownership etc.

30   Maintain the right to invite tenders for new work.

31   Recognise that requirements will change and be willing to adjust costs accordingly.

32   Ensure that SLAs are always realistic and do not expect them to remain static (see Section 5).

33   Continue to benchmark the service and consider alternative approaches.

34   Discuss with all concerned, at the earliest possible stage, plans which could affect services.

Communication/Understanding Issues

35   Clearly define the scope and interfaces of what is outsourced.

36   Establish unambiguous roles and responsibilities for the customer, end-users and supplier (see Appendix 4).

37   Maintain regular customer/supplier contact at various levels – even when things are going well.

38   Establish an open relationship – be prepared to compromise.

39   Build a relationship of trust with the supplier.

40   Hold regular meetings to monitor achievements (see Section 6).

41   Define clear escalation procedures.

42   Do not abuse escalation procedures – nit picking with managers is counter productive.

43   Encourage the supplier to propose changes based on their expertise.

44   Ensure customer awareness, understanding and commitment.

3 Guidelines - Explanatory Notes

Introduction

3.1 This section contains a brief explanation of each of the Guidelines contained in Section 2.

3.2 The Guidelines are categorised as in Section 2 (Management, Human Resource, Service/Business and Communication/Understanding) and appear in the same sequence.

3.3 Each entry consists of a brief explanation, together with summaries of the benefits to be gained from adhering to the guideline and the risks of non-adherence. In many cases actions are suggested which would help towards following the Guideline. Many of the Guidelines are complementary to each other; cross references are given to such related entries.

3.4 This document is aimed at busy managers. It is anticipated that on the first perusal the reader may wish to read this section in its entirety; thereafter, it is expected to be used merely to refresh the memory, with Section 2 providing the key reference points.

3.5 Refer to the Definition of Terms which follows the introduction to Section 2.

MANAGEMENT ISSUES

1

Retain in-house control over strategic direction

Explanation: The strategic direction of an organisation's IS is key to its overall goals and aims. IS strategy should be closely aligned to Business Strategy and setting and controlling strategic direction is a fundamental core competency which should remain within the business.

Benefits: The IS future direction will be set and controlled by business stakeholders who will use their knowledge and judgement to ensure that the IS strategy properly serves the future needs of the business.

Risks: Handing over the responsibility for IS strategic direction to a service company which may not understand the business direction may lead to decisions being made which (much later) prove restrictive or even damaging to business options and direction.

Suggestions: In the contract make it clear that strategy will be set by the customer. Ensure that top management fully support this decision and its implications, and that key strategy personnel are retained.
See also: Guideline 21.

2   Retain responsibility for setting standards to which the supplier must conform

Explanation:

It is essential to retain the right to define both the levels of service quality, security, etc. and the technology interfaces (if any) required of the supplier. The setting of standards is the key tool which the customer can use to keep control over its suppliers.

Benefits:

The judicious application of both technical and management standards can help to create a service environment which is stable, predictable and measurable. A consistent set of standards applied to services taken from different suppliers will enable the services to be integrated seamlessly. Services would be able to be transferred to another supplier or brought in house at a later date.

Risks:

Allowing suppliers to set their own (different) standards could make the later integration of services very costly. Handing over the responsibility for technical standard setting to one supplier could lead to lock-in (and lock-out of other suppliers). Allowing a supplier to set their own performance standards could let them go for the soft option.

Suggestions:

Keep in-house and outsourced standards in step. Review standards at regular intervals and, in collaboration with suppliers, be willing to adjust standards if better solutions are possible. Apply consistent standards to all outsourcing suppliers.

3   Use a prime contractor

Explanation: Where more than one supplier is involved (e.g. hardware / software maintainers, software suppliers, operators, telecommunications staff etc) - it is advisable to vest authority for the overall service in one supplier who is then responsible for managing the others.

Benefits: The effort required for problem management is minimised; communication paths are simplified; the onus for problem diagnosis and attribution is removed from the customer to the (prime) supplier; monitoring service quality is simplified.

Risks: If suppliers of different services are managed directly by the customer, resolution of problems may be greatly delayed by difficulties in attributing responsibility and by conflict between suppliers, leading to customer dissatisfaction. It would also open the door to allow suppliers to play off against each other when awkward problems arise.

Suggestions: There may be no need to follow this guideline if the combination of suppliers is easy to manage. Use this arrangement to simplify the integration of future new services. Ensure that the prime contractor accepts responsibility for service delivery to the end-users. Ensure that other suppliers accept the role of the prime supplier. As far as possible, guard against lock-in to the prime contractor.
See also: Guideline 7

4 Make the supplier responsible for delivery

Explanation: Ensure that the supplier is responsible for delivery of the service at the point of use within the client organisation (i.e. to the "end-user" who has the greatest interest in high-quality service). A particular example would be to give the supplier responsibility for installing / maintaining / managing telecommunications facilities used for the delivery of on-line services.

Benefits: Contract management overheads are reduced by making the supplier responsible for delivery to the end-user. The end-user is in the best position to monitor service quality; supplier staff are likely to build better relationships with the end-users.

Risks: If end-users are not directly involved in monitoring services there is a danger that there will be a delay in the detection of deteriorating services.

Suggestions: Ensure that end-users and the supplier accept that the supplier has responsibility for delivery. Ensure that delivery performance is monitored.
See also: Guideline 26.

5

Be prescriptive about the service requirements rather than the method of service delivery

Explanation: The contract should include specific statements, requirements and targets which spell out exactly what levels of service the supplier is required to deliver to the customer.

Benefits: The supplier may identify opportunities to vary the method of service delivery over time without detracting from the level of service provided to the customer (e.g. downsizing to smaller processors). By making it absolutely clear at the contract stage what the service requirements are, the supplier and customer will have the same expectations. By not including any statements about the method, the contract will leave the supplier scope to introduce their own solutions and improvements.

Risks: Being prescriptive about the method of delivery may cause the supplier to miss opportunities to introduce changes which improve the service to the customer. It could create a relationship where the supplier is discouraged from being pro-active. It also leaves the customer with the responsibility for investigating and keeping abreast of opportunities for improvement.

Suggestions: Ensure that the end-users and business management buy-in to the requirements statements. Do not concentrate on the technicalities of how service levels should be met. Regularly assess customer service level requirements and agree service variations with the supplier as necessary. *See also: Guideline 31*

IMPACT OUTSOURCING
GUIDELINE

6   Never lose sight of the business driven objectives of outsourcing

Explanation: Outsourcing is a means to an end (e.g. cost reduction, concentration on core business), not an end in itself. Outsourced activities should be reviewed regularly to ensure that they continue to make an effective contribution to the organisation's goals, without constraining it unnecessarily.

Benefits: Having continuous focus on the basic business objectives should increase the chances of actually achieving them. Keeping this orientation should help to retain the attention and support of key business sponsors of IS.

Risks: Losing business focus may lead to deterioration of the service to end-users. It would also make it difficult to retain end-user and business management commitment and interest which are vital to making the service a success.

Suggestions: Involve the end-users and business management in the formulation and review of the business objectives of the outsourcing contract. Conduct end-user satisfaction surveys to ensure that end-user requirements are being met.

7 Avoid lock-in to a single supplier

Explanation: Over dependence on an outsourcing supplier can make the costs and risks of moving to another supplier unacceptably high. This in turn reduces the pressure which can be brought to bear on the existing supplier, either to reduce costs or should service quality deteriorate.

Benefits: Control: the availability of the option to switch to an alternative supplier enables greater pressure to be brought to bear in any subsequent negotiations. Flexibility: it is possible to put the service to tender in later years, offering potential cost reductions and the opportunity to take advantage of better offerings which may appear in the market place after the initial contract is placed.

Risks: Being locked-in increases risk from supplier failure. Knowing that there are no easy alternatives may allow the supplier to take advantage of you over cost and quality.

Suggestions: Retain a good understanding of the outsourced function (both by strong contract management and, if appropriate, by retaining scarce and essential technical expertise). Include contract clauses committing the supplier to provide assistance and information upon contract termination. Where appropriate, retain ownership of physical assets whose operation is being transferred to the supplier. Ensure that the supplier adheres to your standards.
See also: Guidelines 2, 3, 15, 29 and 30.

8 Expect value for money but accept the supplier's need to make a profit - a partnership

Explanation: Take a balanced view when negotiating with suppliers. Most contracts are for a long period and success will rely on both parties being able to achieve business benefits.

Benefits: Creating a partnership should increase the commitment of both parties and increase the chances of success. Both parties should be able to understand and respect the other's needs and desires.

Risks: Creating a "win - lose" situation with a supplier will lead to resentment and loss of commitment. It could also impose a confrontational rather than a co-operational style.

Suggestions: Let the supplier share the benefits and they will more readily identify potential improvements and economies. Recognise the supplier's need to make a reasonable profit.
See also: Guidelines 38 and 43.

9 Understand the strategic, political and managerial implications of the scope of your outsourcing

Explanation: Put outsourcing into the "big picture" of your organisation. Do not treat it as a back room technical activity. It will affect responsibilities, relationships and `the way we work' over a wide front.

Benefits: Good communication and setting of expectations at the time of announcement, including areas not directly affected by the decision, will increase the likelihood of rapid acceptance and minimise both the need for damage limitation and the risk of non-co-operation by business management and staff.

Risks: Excessive management effort may be required to overcome customer resistance to outsourcing; the relationship may be inadequately managed, causing service quality to suffer and outsourcing activities to be perceived as unsuccessful.

Suggestions: Plan for and accommodate the knock-on effects of any outsourcing decision. Consider strategic issues: Is the function being outsourced "core", critical, important or peripheral to the main business? Will outsourcing increase or reduce the options available for future strategic decision making, for this and / or other related functions? Consider political issues: What will be the reaction of directors, shareholders, unions, management and staff elsewhere in the organisation? (e.g. will staff in other functions perceive themselves as threatened?) Consider managerial issues: How many levels of management will be outsourced? How will the supplier be managed by the business manager or end-user, and at what level? How will that management interface with management elsewhere in the organisation? *See also: Guideline 44.*

IMPACT OUTSOURCING
GUIDELINE

10   Define supplier's points of contact - ensure adherence

Explanation: Be specific so that the supplier (and the contacts) know exactly what is expected of them. Stop the supplier from by-passing the nominated customer contact structure.

Benefits: Regular points of contact with defined terms of reference will help the supplier give the right level of attention to key individuals. Enforcement of the points of contact will stop the supplier making unwanted overtures to senior management. The contact points will also be clear about their own responsibilities.

Risks: Without this clarity - the supplier may be able to bypass and undermine the customer contacts. The end-users of the service and other key individuals may become isolated and disillusioned. The supplier may try to shift focus away from the core of the service to pursue other more lucrative opportunities.

Suggestions: Build the formal contact structure into the contract. Monitor the supplier to ensure compliance.
See also: Guidelines 4, 14, 41 and 44.

IMPACT OUTSOURCING
GUIDELINE

11 Having an appropriate person to manage the contract is key (see Section 4)

Explanation: The management of the contract is key to the success of outsourcing. The person who takes responsibility for this must be carefully selected and briefed.

Benefits: Having the right blend of knowledge, attitude and skill will help to keep the relationship between supplier and customer working smoothly. The confidence of the business managers and end-users will increase if the contract is managed by someone they trust. The supplier will take notice of someone who has wide support and high credibility.

Risks: A contract manager with the wrong attributes could quickly destroy the relationship with the supplier. A manager who did not have the support of business managers and end-users could be undermined by the supplier.

Suggestions: Identify the Customer Contract Manager at the earliest possible date and involve this manager in the supplier evaluation and selection process. *See also: Guideline 24.*

IMPACT OUTSOURCING
GUIDELINE

12 Keep the procedures simple

Explanation: All support, monitoring and change control procedures must be made as simple and as explicit as possible so that there is no doubt about exactly what is required.

Benefits: Simple procedures will reduce the cost of monitoring and managing the contract. Everyone will be able to understand exactly what is expected of them. The easier the procedure is - the more likely it will actually be carried out.

Risks: Complex procedures may lead to increased confusion and disputes. If procedures seem over-complex - they are likely to be short-circuited or bypassed completely. Enforcing over-complex procedures will lead to unnecessary cost and effort and eventual disillusionment of end-users and the supplier.

Suggestions: Build automatic measurement and monitoring into the day to day procedures.
Avoid complex manual data collection and analysis. Encourage supplier self-monitoring.

13

Regularly review the outsourcing contract and
relationship with the supplier

Explanation: Set and stick to regular formal reviews of the contract. Hold these even if
things are going well.

Benefits: This will indicate to the supplier that you are serious and will enable you
to focus away from the detail. It will enable both sides to raise key issues
and concerns which affect the overall relationship.

Risks: Without this type of forum - important trends and non-specific key issues
may be overlooked. The supplier may be able to meet all the detailed
performance measures whilst at the same time not providing a
satisfactory overall relationship.

Suggestions: Separate these from reviews of the specific service level agreements.
Involve your senior business managers and end-users in steering and
shaping the relationship.
See also: Guidelines 17 and 19.

IMPACT OUTSOURCING
GUIDELINE

14   Never stop negotiating

Explanation: Do not assume that once the contract is agreed that negotiation is over. In order to keep the service relevant and effective it will be necessary to continue to negotiate for improvements and changes.

Benefits: Continual negotiation will keep the contract alive. It will be clear to the supplier and your end-users that there will always be opportunities for implementing improvements. The chances of getting the contract exactly right first time are remote, negotiation and renegotiation should become the accepted practice.

Risks: Without the culture of continuous negotiation the supplier may get flabby and relaxed. It may be more difficult to get the supplier to accept changes and improvements to the contract. Also, the customer may cease to question service requirements and expectations; opportunities for improvement may be missed.

Suggestions: Ensure that the variable SLAs are separated from the main body of the contract but are clearly part of the binding agreement. Ensure that SLAs can be added and amended with relative ease. Be prepared to negotiate at different management levels with the supplier (from the Supplier Contract Manager up to the Managing Director).

IMPACT OUTSOURCING
GUIDELINE

15   Re-tender contracts at defined intervals

Explanation: Make it clear to the supplier that the contract will be put out to re-tender at predefined intervals. Ensure that this is actually carried out.

Benefits: The supplier will understand that it is not a contract for life. The formal re-tender process will act as a good discipline to confirm that the business objectives and aims have not changed. It also provides the opportunity to test the supplier against the marketplace both for value for money and for quality of service.

Risks: If the contract is not re-tendered then you may never know if you are over paying for the service. The opportunity to gain advantage by using new suppliers with new ideas may also be lost.

Suggestions: Ensure that the original contract allows for the re-tendering process. Do not under- estimate the effort involved in re-tendering (both customer and supplier) Try to find fast tracks through the re-tendering process.

16 Regularly review the outsourcing market to identify trends and changes

Explanation: The outsourcing market is growing and changing rapidly with many new services and suppliers being introduced. It is important to keep in touch with these changes and a formal regular review process should be introduced.

Benefits: Reviewing the marketplace will enable you to maintain your awareness of current best practice. This will improve your ability to manage your supplier. If your supplier knows that you intend to conduct regular reviews they will be more likely to ensure that they keep the service up to date.

Risks: Without knowledge of the external marketplace you will not know whether your supplier and contract are still providing value for money.

Suggestions: Maintain contact with other outsource service suppliers and customers.
See also: Guideline 33.

IMPACT OUTSOURCING
GUIDELINE

17

Monitor supplier's resource levels and business knowledge

Explanation: Keep the initiative by formally and regularly conducting reviews of the supplier to ensure that they can still provide the level of support and cover which you require.

Benefits: The reviews will enable you to spot potential problems in advance. The supplier will also understand that the continued availability of skilled resources is important.

Risks: The supplier may try to move in the "B team". The supplier may cut back until they are only just able to meet service levels.

Suggestions: Look for signs of the supplier's continuing commitment to the contract. Monitor the quality and the knowledge levels of supplier staff.
See also: Guideline 27.

18 Encourage co-operative contract evolution to take advantage of developing technologies

Explanation: The contract should be worded and managed so that all opportunities for improving the service are in the interests of both parties.

Benefits: Throughout the life of the contract, many new technology opportunities will arise. Those which can provide benefit to both supplier and customer will be able to be included. This could lead to cost savings or improvements in service to end-users.

Risks: Having a contract which does not encourage technology changes may lead to cost saving opportunities being lost. A contract which allows no technology changes at all will eventually lead to escalating support costs and disillusioned end-users. The supplier may be aware of potential improvements but will not implement them.

Suggestions: Ensure that the agreement enables improved technology to be readily adopted.
See also: Guidelines 2, 5, 43 and 44.

19
Retain and exercise the right to conduct IS audits at supplier's premises

Explanation: Establish your contractual right to examine all relevant aspects of the supplier's operations. Set a timetable for regular audits and stick to it.

Benefits: Retaining the right to audit should help to give your end-users peace of mind over issues of security. Conducting regular audits will allow you to check that the supplier is maintaining satisfactory working practices.

Risks: The supplier may lock you in to their own practices. You may inadvertently sign away the rights which your auditors had over the in-house service. Without formal audits your supplier may adopt risky or unacceptable working practices - and you may be unaware.

Suggestions: Inspect the supplier's methods and practices. Follow through the supplier's audit trails and security procedures.
See also: Guideline 7.

20   Aim for continuous improvement

Explanation: A culture of continuously seeking improvements (in the cost and quality of the service) should be instilled into the supplier and the end-users.

Benefits: If everyone connected with the service is continually looking to improve it then it is likely that it will actually improve. This culture helps to improve customer and end-user focus, and challenges and motivates all those connected with delivering and using the service.

Risks: Opportunities for incremental improvements could be overlooked or ignored. Supplier and end-user staff may not be motivated to pursue ideas for improvement. You may fall so far behind that you are forced to change supplier.

Suggestions: Staff should be empowered to implement the improvements which they have identified. A method of sharing the rewards should be devised. Managers should be seeking ways to benchmark services to ensure that the supplier keeps up with market trends in cost/performance.
See also: Guidelines 15, 18 and 33.

HUMAN RESOURCE ISSUES

21

Ensure sufficient number and quality of in-house staff remain to manage the outsourced situation (see Section 4)

Explanation: Take care to ensure that the skills required to carry out the functions which are to remain in-house are identified and that appropriate staff are retained.

Benefits: The organisation will have the resources to successfully manage the contract and the supplier, and the skills required to control the IS strategy and set standards.

Risks: Without staff with the necessary qualities and skills it will be difficult to manage the contract and the supplier effectively. The supplier may be able to manipulate the end-users. The organisation may lose the ability to develop its IS strategy, and gradually become more dependant on supplier staff expertise.

Suggestions: To ensure the continued availability of the required skills consider a "Loyalty Bonus" scheme for key personnel and perhaps build secondment programs. This could be two way - the organisation gains IS experience, your supplier gains experience of your business. Required technical skills could be bought in.
See also: Guidelines 1, 2, 17, 25 and 38.

22   Promote a continuing bond between supplier staff and end-users

Explanation: Initially this will happen by default if your staff have transferred to the supplier , but it is important to encourage friendly working relationships to continue and new ones to develop.

Benefits: Good working relationships should result in the supplier having an increased ability to understand end-user requirements and problems which should lead to more effective systems. Increased contact should give the end-users increased IT awareness, and, in turn, lead to increased involvement in and ownership of the systems by the end-users.

Risks: An "Us and Them" feeling could develop which would lead to less effective end-user support services, for example: Help Desk, Application Support. The end-users would feel that they lacked control and ownership of the systems.

Suggestions: A programme of liaison visits or a secondment program could be used to encourage working relationships.
See also: Guidelines 21 and 23.

IMPACT OUTSOURCING
GUIDELINE

23   Make morale of supplier staff a customer concern

Explanation: This is most applicable when your staff have transferred to the supplier organisation, but it is still an issue with existing supplier staff. It should apply as soon as negotiations begin.

Benefits: Happy, well motivated staff within the supplier organisation will provide a better service to your end-users. Increased morale will lead to greater stability and continuity amongst the supplier staff which will allow skill levels and experience to be maintained.

Risks: A high staff turnover within the supplier would lead to a decrease in the service quality.

Suggestions: During the negotiation phase get a feel for the "culture" within the supplier organisation: how do they treat their existing staff? Ensure that the supplier management, and any transferring staff, know that staff morale is important to you.

IMPACT OUTSOURCING
GUIDELINE

24 Sort out personality conflicts as soon as possible

Explanation: Whatever the contract may say, personality conflicts can be extremely damaging, a great deal of change is taking place and lots of new relationships must be established; try to ensure none of them is soured.

Benefits: Good personal relationships are more productive, people will work together to produce better solutions. If individual working relationships are good between the two organisations there will be an increased chance of a partnership attitude developing.

Risks: Personality conflicts between staff in key roles would make managing the contract effectively very difficult. The confrontational stance could permeate to other relationships.

Suggestions: Encourage openness within the organisations, avoid a "blame" culture. Listen and be aware of potential problems. Be prepared to move "difficult" in-house staff and expect the supplier to do the same.

25 Regularly review in-house staff skills and numbers

Explanation: The number of in-house staff and the skills that will be required may change as the contract evolves.

Benefits: By regularly reviewing this situation, the organisation will be able to anticipate skill shortages or mismatches before there is any impact on performance in, for example: contract management, strategy development, or end-user services.

Risks: If skill levels and numbers do not keep pace with changing requirements there could be difficulties managing the contract with the supplier. The organisation could become increasingly dependant on the expertise of supplier staff.

Suggestions: Identify early the skills required and the training necessary as the contract evolves and ensure that the training is undertaken.
See also: Guideline 21.

IMPACT OUTSOURCING
GUIDELINE

26   Involve end-users in monitoring service delivery against targets (see Section 6)

Explanation: The end-users are best placed as users and owners of the services to monitor their delivery.

Benefits: The organisation will get a fuller picture of the supplier's performance, and the importance of the end-users will be reinforced within the supplier organisation. The end-user is better able to identify mismatches between SLAs and his requirements.

Risks: The supplier may otherwise, unwittingly perhaps, give a false picture of his performance. The supplier will be less quickly aware of changing end-user needs.

Suggestions: Ensure that appropriate performance indicators have been agreed and that the monitoring of these is simple, automatic if possible. Ensure that there are regular meetings between the Customer's Contract Manager and the end-users. Involve end-users in review meetings.
See also: Guideline 4.

27

Retain the right to veto supplier's choice of key staff.

Explanation: Key staff have difficult and demanding jobs, the organisation must satisfy itself that any replacements the supplier proposes for key positions have the necessary skills and experience. An organisation may have specific security requirements for supplier staff.

Benefits: The quality of service delivered by the supplier should be maintained throughout the life of the contract. The right supplier staff should ensure good working relationships with both end-users and contract management team.

Risks: The inexperience of supplier staff could reduce service quality, the supplier could gradually introduce his "B Team" to service your contract. Damaging personality conflicts would be difficult to resolve.

Suggestions: Make it clear from the outset what your expectations are and ensure that the key roles are identified in the contract. Ensure, where possible, you are given early warning of projected supplier staff changes.
See also: Guidelines 17 and 24.

SERVICE/BUSINESS ISSUES

28

Match expectations with needs, not historical achievements

Explanation: The end-users will be accustomed to a particular level of service, which may not be what they actually want or need. As a general rule the level of service should be at least equal to that currently delivered unless there is good reason for lower service levels and the agreed levels are well understood.

Benefits: The organisation will get a service matched to current end-user requirements.

Risks: The organisation could pay for a (level of) service that is no longer required.

Suggestions: The organisation should manage the end-users' expectations, ensure that the cost implications of requirements are understood by the end-users and help them to analyse their requirements carefully.

IMPACT OUTSOURCING
GUIDELINE

29

Have a contingency escape plan covering the outsourcing contract, software ownership etc

Explanation: The organisation must ensure that mutually agreed termination mechanisms are included in the contract and that software licences and other agreements do not carry financial penalties for a change of outsourcing supplier or reversion in-house.

Benefits: If things go wrong or circumstances change the mutually agreed mechanisms can be invoked in a timely way.

Risks: Ending an unhappy marriage can be a very long drawn-out, costly affair, the organisation could find itself locked-in to the supplier. Prolonged difficulties will adversely affect the service quality delivered by the supplier.

Suggestions: The organisation should ensure that invocation circumstances are agreed with the supplier and defined in the contract.
See also: Guideline 7.

30   Maintain the right to invite tenders for new work

Explanation: The existing supplier cannot expect to get new work from the organisation without it being the subject of competition. However, be aware that multiple contracts may be more difficult to manage. A prime contractor may become necessary.

Benefits: Retaining the right to subject new services to competition will help ensure value for money and will give the organisation flexibility to use the market. The possibility of competition will encourage the existing supplier to provide continuous improvement.

Risks: The existing supplier may see the organisation as a captive market and overcharge for new services. The organisation may find itself increasingly locked-in to the supplier. The supplier, in turn, may become complacent and service quality may suffer.

Suggestions: The organisation should ensure that all service boundaries are clearly defined in the contract, in order that there can be no disagreement on what would constitute an enhancement and what new work.
See also: Guidelines 3 and 33.

31

Recognise that requirements will change and be willing to adjust costs accordingly

Explanation:

The organisation should recognise that requirements will change during the life of the contract and should expect to pay more for enhanced or new services (or conversely less for reduced services).

Benefits:

As the business evolves the organisation continues to get the services that meet its needs. IS continues to be an enabler not a constraint to the business.

Risks:

The services as originally specified may no longer match business requirements. The business may not be able to evolve as required due to IS constraints.

Suggestions:

The organisation should ensure that mutually agreed change mechanisms are included in the contract. The business requirements and the services provided should be regularly reviewed so that necessary changes can be identified as soon as possible.

See also: Guideline 34.

32

Ensure that SLAs are always realistic and do not expect them to remain static (see Section 5)

Explanation: An SLA is a negotiated agreement between the supplier and the end-user of a service, as such it must be achievable and meet reasonable requirements. As the business and technologies evolve what is required and what is achievable will change.

Benefits: The organisation will get levels of service matched to current end-user requirements. The level of service can evolve as the business evolves. The supplier will be more committed if the objectives are realistic.

Risks: The organisation could pay for a level of service that is no longer required. The business may not gain the full benefit of service improvements made possible by newer or cheaper technologies.

Suggestions: The organisation should agree a process for SLA re-negotiation with the supplier and include it in the contract. To aid the understanding of future expectations, include an indication of future service goals in the SLA. *See also: Guideline 14.*

33

Continue to benchmark the services and consider alternative approaches

Explanation: Markets and technologies evolve, benchmarking can provide a basis for continuous improvement. The organisation should ensure that the benchmarking methodologies to be used are agreed beforehand with the supplier.

Benefits: Benchmarking will provide a measure of the quality of service and value for money you are getting from the supplier. It will give the organisation a lever to use in discussions with the supplier and will encourage the continuous improvement of services.

Risks: The organisation will have no comparative data to indicate whether the supplier is continuing to provide a competitive, high quality service. The organisation will become increasingly reliant on the supplier's estimates of costs for new or enhanced services.

Suggestions: Ensure that the supplier participates in the benchmarking process. The contract should be written to include provision for re-negotiation should the gap between benchmarked and supplier services exceed an agreed margin.

See also: Guidelines 16, 18, 20, 30 and 32.

34

Discuss with all concerned, at the earliest possible stage, plans which could affect services

Explanation: Your business and therefore your requirements will not remain static. The supplier should be involved at all levels in the planning processes concerning areas that could affect the services he is providing.

Benefits: Major changes may require lengthy contract re-negotiation, the sooner this can be started the better. The service provider may have valuable input with regard to the viability, costs etc of the various options under consideration. The supplier will need sufficient time to properly implement the required changes.

Risks: Required changes may be delayed if the supplier is unable to meet the requirements at short notice, or may be very costly to achieve in the required timescales.

Suggestions: Include provision in the contract for supplier representation at reviews at specified management levels. Specify the frequency of such meetings between the customer, the supplier and business management and end-users as necessary.
See also: Guideline 31.

COMMUNICATION/UNDERSTANDING ISSUES

35

Clearly define the scope and interfaces of what is outsourced

Explanation: There needs to be a clear understanding of which activities are to be outsourced and which retained in-house.

Benefits: Clear boundaries for outsourcing contracts along with clear roles and responsibilities reduce confusion, cost and risk.

Risks: If the scope of what is outsourced is not clear, unexpected costs may arise as extra services have to be added to the contract. IS provision covers a wide range of activities and outsourcing may be pursued through the letting of one contract or several; without clear boundaries suppliers may duplicate work, or requirements may fall between the stools.

Suggestions: Take a strategic view of outsourcing; identify services that will and will not be outsourced. Clearly define interfaces between different suppliers - for example, between software developers and operational service suppliers. Consider using a prime contractor.
See also: Guidelines 3 and 9.

40   Hold regular meetings to monitor achievements (see Section 6)

Explanation: The success of outsourcing is greatly influenced by the nature of the relationship between customer and supplier. Distinct roles and responsibilities can be identified for the end-user of the service, the supplier, and the customer.

Benefits: Clearly defined roles and responsibilities reduce duplication and cost, and result in better working relationships.

Risks: If responsibilities are unclear, confusion may arise and the customer may find that unexpected costs are incurred. There is a risk that the customers or end-users will duplicate the activities of the supplier.

Suggestions: Establish roles and responsibilities during the outsourcing negotiations. Identify and publicise internal responsibilities, including the roles of business managers, end-users and the customer's Contract Manager. Document procedures and lines of communication in a Code of Practice for the outsourced services.
See also: Guidelines 4 and 10.

IMPACT OUTSOURCING
GUIDELINE

37 Maintain regular customer/supplier contact at various levels – even when things are going well

Explanation: Procedures should be defined which set out appropriate channels of communication between the customer, end-users and supplier. These contacts should not be limited to discussions about problems, but should also address plans, opportunities, reviews of success.

Benefits: Regular contacts help to foster good working relationships and anticipate changes. Discussing plans may provide opportunities to exploit supplier knowledge and skills, and reduce costs.

Risks: Allowing regular contact between the customer, end-users and supplier to fade away, perhaps because things appear to be going well, may mean that problems which do arise will not be detected or will be harder to resolve due to lack of good relationships. Limiting contact to discussions of problems encourages a negative attitude to the contract

Suggestions: Identify contacts at various levels, for example: between senior supplier and business managers to discuss strategic business direction; and regular (weekly/monthly) service performance reviews. Plan a regular schedule of meetings.
See also: Guidelines 13, 14, 34 and 40.

38

Establish an open relationship – be prepared to compromise

Explanation: The customer and supplier will, inevitably, have different perspectives; but that need not preclude good communication or obstruct a sound relationship. A degree of give and take is needed.

Benefits: Openness encourages a shared determination to make the contract work. The contract is more likely to be able to develop - outsourcing contracts often cover a long period in which customer requirements may change - if the relationship is good.

Risks: The customer and supplier may fail to recognise or exploit common interests and opportunities. A determination never to compromise may sour relationships.

Suggestions: Accept differences in perspective but share concerns, plans and information through regular contact. Encourage a culture and an approach to the contract which emphasise co-operation rather than antagonism. Consider the scope for `open book' approaches whereby the supplier makes his costs known to the customer to a greater or lesser extent.
See also: Guidelines 8 and 14.

IMPACT OUTSOURCING
GUIDELINE

39

Build a relationship of trust with the supplier

Explanation: Many organisations express concerns about losing control and about the risk of being exploited by an unscrupulous supplier. In contrast, companies with successful outsourcing experiences emphasise the importance of trust between the customer and supplier.

Benefits: Both parties are more likely to be honest about what is required and about what they can offer. As trust develops over time, the customer may be content to reduce resources committed to monitoring performance and involve suppliers more in internal discussions and planning.

Risks: There may be a tendency to assume an antagonistic attitude; both the supplier and the customer may seek opportunities to exploit each other rather than seek mutual benefits. Emphasising detailed monitoring of the supplier's working practices may increase the customer's costs. Without trust the customer is unlikely to share information with the supplier and, as a result, opportunities for improvement may be missed.

Suggestions: Express a wish to develop trust during negotiation and give the supplier opportunities to earn it (the supplier must, as a minimum, meet agreed targets). Acknowledge good performance; be open about concerns.
See also: Guidelines 8, 22 and 42.

36   Establish unambiguous roles and responsibilities for the customer, end-users and supplier (see Appendix 4)

Explanation: Regular meetings between the customer and supplier are required to monitor progress and to discuss problems and changes, plans and proposals.

Benefits: Meetings supplement performance reporting and help to build relationships, and support timely anticipation of problems and changes.

Risks: Relationships may drift. Failure to spot problems, trends, and opportunities.

Suggestions: Set up meetings to reflect the various forms and levels of customer/supplier contact. For example, weekly or monthly meetings to review service performance; quarterly or biannual meetings of senior managers to discuss strategy and plans. Ensure meetings are not onerous or overly bureaucratic - keep to clear objectives and timescales.
See also: Guidelines 13, 34 and 37.

41   Define clear escalation procedures

Explanation: However good the relationship between customer and supplier, problems may arise. So procedures should be agreed for handling problems.

Benefits: Responsibilities and levels of authority are clear. Customer and supplier co-operate to ensure that problems are recognised and then resolved quickly and efficiently. Clear problem reporting and escalation procedures help keep the heat out of the relationship.

Risks: Without clear escalation procedures, end-users may not know how to raise problems which means they will take longer to resolve, cost more and cause more inconvenience. This, in turn, worsens end-user perceptions of the service.

Suggestions: Define escalation procedures in the contract; use them when necessary. Allow for successive levels of response depending on the nature of the problem and the outcome of action taken at lower levels. Try to resolve problems at the lowest practicable level. Ensure people have appropriate levels of authority to resolve problems. Define timescales for escalating problems - this provides a discipline for the process.
See also: Guideline 10.

42   Do not abuse escalation procedures

Explanation: Some customers believe the best way to deal with problems is to address them all to the Managing Director of the supplier organisation. But agreed escalation procedures should be followed.

Benefits: Problems get solved at the lowest level possible, quickly and with minimum fuss. When there are serious problems, escalation carries weight.

Risks: Bypassing agreed escalation routes inhibits the development of trust; sours working relationships; and can undermine the authority of supplier staff who could and should deal with the problem. And when there are major issues to resolve, their importance may not be recognised.

Suggestions: Don't cry "wolf" unnecessarily! Ensure all parties are familiar with the escalation procedures. Monitor problems and how well the escalation procedures deal with them.

IMPACT OUTSOURCING
GUIDELINE

43

Encourage the supplier to propose changes based on their expertise

Explanation: There may be opportunities which the supplier will identify, perhaps based on experiences with other outsourcing contracts or expertise in other services or technologies.

Benefits: Encouraging the supplier to make proposals may offer opportunities to improve the customer's business, to improve existing services or to cut costs.

Risks: Missed opportunity to benefit from the supplier's accumulated knowledge.

Suggestions: Consider offering incentives for the supplier to make innovative proposals; for example, allowing some sharing of the resulting benefits. Ensure that in all cases the final decision on whether to pursue changes rests with the customer.
See also: Guidelines 2, 8, 14 and 18.

IMPACT OUTSOURCING
GUIDELINE

44

Ensure customer awareness, understanding and commitment

Explanation: People throughout the customer organisation need to be aware of the decision to outsource and need to understand the impact it will have.

Benefits: If business managers and end-users understand the reasons for outsourcing and the impact it will have, such as new ways of working, outsourcing is more likely to be successful.

Risks: Failing to inform business managers and end-users about the outsourcing contract can generate resentment and can lead to confusion. Activities may be duplicated and failure to follow new procedures or meet customer obligations may mean the supplier is unable to provide the agreed service.

Suggestions: Document and publicise the scope and provisions of the contract including any customer obligations. Keep business managers and end-users aware of progress throughout the outsourcing process (while respecting commercial confidentiality). Consider using newsletters, posters, leaflets and presentations. Describe procedures in a code of practice for the outsourced services and make it available to all business managers and end-users. Conduct customer satisfaction surveys.
See also: Guidelines 9, 10 and 28.

4 General Characteristics of Customer and Supplier Contract Managers

4.1 Introduction

Good contract management requires a sound business understanding (a partnership) between the customer and the supplier. Experience shows that a prerequisite for this relationship is having clear responsibilities and lines of communication between the customer's Contract Manager and his opposite number in the supplier organisation. The general attributes required by these two key managers – the two sides of the same coin – are outlined in this Section.

4.2 The Customer's Contract or Relationship Manager

The title Contract Manager is used throughout this report as being a suitably descriptive title which several of the organisations represented on the Working Group are familiar with. Vaughn Hovey, Manager, IT Supplier and Relationship Management for Eastman Kodak Company, suggested the title `Relationship Manager' would be more descriptive of the actual role that should be being performed. Readers may have their own preferences.

4.2.1 *Personality & Key Skills*

An outgoing manager with plenty of confidence, high credibility, determination, self-motivation, pragmatism and flexibility. May have a technical or business background, but must be creative, have broad technical and financial understanding, and excellent communication and negotiation skills.

4.2.2 *Customer Facing*

Has sympathetic views of customer needs based on a good understanding of business requirements. Needs good judgement to know what is and is not realistic and a high level of authority and political skill to retain support and confidence of business managers and end-users.

4.2.3 *Supplier Facing*

Can establish a good rapport with other people generally while maintaining the principles of delivery. Able to bring technical or business argument to bear broadly and specifically. Can deal authoritatively with senior people from the supplier organisation. Being a barrack room lawyer will not help - but a sound understanding of the contract and schedules is needed. A tough, fair negotiator.

4.2.4 *Project Management*

Good understanding of Project Management, methodology, structures, use of tools and estimating; will know almost instinctively whether estimates are reasonable and when actuals are excessive. Requires a sound awareness of business issues which underpin business cases, and how to establish cost controls.

4.2.5 *Quality Monitor*

Needs a questioning mind and must not be afraid to expose gaps in knowledge by asking `simplistic' questions. Challenges issues and solutions and understands how solutions fit into the overall structure. Needs a good balance of strategic and tactical viewpoints.

4.2.6 *Technical Skills*

Good technical awareness of the industry and ability to grasp new areas of technology quickly and accurately and apply them to the business environment.

4.2.7 *Other Attributes*

Trusted by the business managers, end-users and suppliers, and able to act even-handedly between them whilst protecting customer interest.

4.3 The Supplier's Contract Manager

4.3.1 *Personality & Key Skills*

An outgoing manager with plenty of confidence, high credibility, determination, self-motivation, pragmatism and flexibility. May have a technical or business background, but must be creative, have broad technical and financial understanding, and excellent communication and negotiation skills.

4.3.2 *Customer Facing*

Has a good understanding of customer needs and business requirements. Requires good judgement to know what is and is not realistic and a high level of credibility and political skill to retain customer support and confidence.

4.3.3 *Supplier Facing*

Has a very sound knowledge of the organisation and abilities of the supplier and has authority, without reference to others, to instigate effective actions by the supplier. Can establish a good rapport with other people generally while maintaining the principles of delivery. Able to bring technical or business argument to bear broadly and specifically. Requires a sound understanding of the contract and schedules. Must have the authority to negotiate on behalf of the supplier.

4.3.4 *Project Management*

Good understanding of Project Management, methodology, structures, use of tools and estimating; able to provide factual explanations of estimates and actuals as necessary. Requires a sound awareness of business expectations and how to establish cost controls.

4.3.5 *Quality Monitor*

Needs a questioning and challenging mind and a keenness to provide services which satisfy customer expectations. Will work hard to maintain quality standards and a high level of customer service - most of this work will be within the supplier organisation and not visible to the customer. Tackles issues without delay and understands how solutions fit into the overall structure. Needs a good balance of strategic and tactical viewpoints.

4.3.6 *Technical Skills*

Good technical awareness of the industry and ability to grasp new areas of technology quickly and accurately and apply them to the customer's business environment.

4.3.7 *Other Attributes*

Trusted by the customer and the supplier, and able to act even-handedly between them whilst protecting supplier's interest.

5 Important Elements of Service Level Agreements

(SLAs)

5.1 Introduction

There should be no doubts in the minds of the customer or the supplier about the service level expectations of the out-sourced service. Nor should there be any ambiguity about who is responsible for monitoring the service levels, how these service levels are to be measured and reported and the frequency with which they will be reviewed. Monitoring service levels is an activity which should be rigorous and regular in all circumstances, not just when service problems are being experienced.

SLAs are likely to be volatile, it is therefore preferable to have them referenced by the legal contract rather then embedded in it.

Refer also to Guidelines 14 and 32.

5.2 SLA Definitions

- Each system and service
  - Purpose of the system/service
  - System or service inter-dependencies (e.g. job run sequences)
  - Main customer
  - Security requirements
- Data/transaction volumes
  - Source and volume of information
  - Variations - daily, monthly, peak period etc

5.3 Service expectations and future targets

- Batch start/end time constraints and point of delivery
  - External schedules e.g. BACS processing
- On-line response times by system/service
  - Method of measurement
  - Daily average or % within `x' seconds
  - Peak time average or % within `x' seconds
- Engineer response and repair times for end-user work stations
  - % responses within `x' time
  - % repairs within `x' time
  - Mean time between failures for each type of equipment
- Service availability
  - Maximum number and duration of on-line service interrupts per month
  - Maximum number and duration of batch service interrupts per month

5.4 Responsibilities

- Clearly defined accountability for different types of failure
  - Hardware
  - Environmental
  - Telecommunications
  - Applications
  - Systems software
  - Knock-on effects of user error
- Customer commitments
  - System documentation
  - Data accuracy
  - Staff training
- Who to provide service statistics
  - In what form
  - How often

5.5 Change Management

- How are changes to be managed

5.6 Fault Fixing and Escalation Procedures for End-user Work Stations

- How are problems to be reported
- Response fix/repair times for different types of faults
  - Prime shift
  - Weekends, nights and Bank Holidays
  - Customer points of contact
  - Supplier points of contact
  - Procedures for allocating fault severity
  - Target fix/repair time for each severity level
  - Procedures for changing fault severity
- Who to escalate to and when
  - Means of escalation
  - Points of escalation within the customer organisation
  - Points of escalation within the supplier organisation
  - Actions to be taken as the faults escalate (equipment exchange or remote specialist involvement)

5.7 Service Exceptions

- Compensation (these should be structured to act as an incentive to the supplier to rectify defects, not as a post facto punishment)
- Benchmarking and market awareness should provide the incentive for maintaining high service levels and increasing the likelihood of a long term relationship (see Guidelines 6, 16, 18, 20 and 33).

5.8 Disaster Contingency Arrangements

- Details of the required contingency arrangements
  - How comprehensive
  - How secure
  - What guarantee of availability
  - Maximum duration of use
- Contingency testing arrangements
  - Responsibilities
- Circumstances which will lead to instigating use of disaster/contingency arrangements
- Disaster contingency service expectations
  - Maximum time to recover defined priority services
  - Maximum time to recover other services
  - Performance targets

5.9 Variations

- Circumstances under which requirements may be waived or priorities revised
  e.g. Annual review to assess the opportunities arising from technology advances
  - Changing transaction volumes or number of customers
  - Inclusion of new systems or services
- Process for agreeing changes to SLAs

5.10 Regular Service Reviews

- Frequency of review
- Location of reviews
- Review meeting format and attendees

Notes:
i) The above Guidelines are based on limited analysis and are not claimed to be exhaustive.
ii) Financial considerations are normally contained in the main contract rather than within individual SLAs. However, aspects of the SLAs (e.g. failure to respond to faults within agreed times) may have significant financial implications which must not be overlooked, ie, penalties and incentive payments.

6 Review Meeting Agenda

6.1 The Explanatory Notes in Section 3 for Guidelines 10, 13, 17, 26, 31, 34, 37 and 40 indicate the need for formalised contact with the supplier; in many of the others such a need is implicit.

6.2 Listed below are the items which are recommended to be covered by regular meetings. The list is not exhaustive, but it is unlikely that any of the items given can safely be ignored.

6.3 Although the list is presented as one composite agenda, in most cases it will be more appropriate to hold two or three different types of meeting, each with a subset of the items below. This would enable each topic to be addressed with the right degree of frequency and by the most appropriate levels of staff within the customer and supplier organisations. For example, the following meetings might be held:

i) **A weekly or monthly meeting to review service performance.**
This meeting would be attended by end-users and the supplier's technical managers.

ii) **A quarterly meeting to review services and SLAs.**
This meeting would be attended by business managers, contract managers and the supplier's technical managers.

iii) **A quarterly or biannual meeting to review changes, future plans and financial matters.**
This meeting would be attended by senior business management, contract managers and senior supplier management.

6.4 Where interrelated services are outsourced to more than one supplier, the customer will need to decide which subjects should be discussed individually with each, and which (if any) should be dealt with at meetings involving more than one supplier (see Guideline 3).

6.5 Suggested agenda items for review meetings with suppliers:

1   Minutes of last meeting
2   Actions arising
3   Review of services
    - service performance statistics and metrics
    - number of problems raised
    - number of problems cleared
    - number of problems escalated
    - number of problems outstanding, analysed by date and priority
4   Possible savings/efficiency improvements in service provision
5   Review of projects
6   Review of change controls
    - on-going changes
    - new changes
7. Financial review
8. Future plans (tactical and strategic)
    - customer's business plans
    - customer's IS/IT plans
    - supplier's plans
9   Any other business, eg:
    - benchmarking/market awareness findings
    - results of customer satisfaction surveys
    - security/audit issues
10 Date of next meeting

Appendix 1 How the Guidelines were Developed

1.1 In normal IMPACT style the first meeting of the Outsourcing Working Group was confined to IMPACT Partners and resulted in a frank exchange of views and experiences in a confidential environment. Although it was apparent that the IMPACT Partners had considerable appreciation of outsourcing and could gain much from an exchange of experiences, the meeting concluded that understanding of the subject would be enhanced by involving a wider grouping. Consequently two actions were agreed:

i) To invite representatives from a few non-IMPACT Partner organisations to present and discuss the subject at Working Group meetings.

ii) To prepare a simple outsourcing questionnaire to elicit experience from a much wider audience.

1.2 The first action resulted in valuable contributions from executives representing ABB Transportation, Granada UK Rental and, to provide a supplier's perspective, SHL Systemhouse.

1.3 The Working Group formed a Sub Group to manage the design, issue and analysis of an outsourcing questionnaire. There was a most satisfactory response with completed questionnaires being returned by over 100 companies. The results of this survey were published in an April 1994 report 'IMPACT IT Effectiveness Review - Outsourcing Survey' which was sent to all IMPACT Partners and companies that responded to the questionnaire. Follow-up telephone conversations were held with several responders who had most extensive outsourcing experience or included most interesting comments in the questionnaire.

1.4 As the above activities progressed a wealth of information was gained about how to manage an outsourcing situation. Also, many organisations provided assessments of best and worst consequences of outsourcing based on their experiences. The Working Group members agreed that sufficient information had been gathered from a wide range of organisations to enable best practice guidelines to be established.

1.5 Information was collated in list form from the questionnaires, Working Group discussions and various presentations. This information was considered and agreed by the Outsourcing Working Group which formed a Sub Group to assist with the task of expanding the lists into guidelines and preparing the best practice report. This report is the result.

Appendix 2 Lessons Learnt – Supplier Selection and Tender

1.1 This Appendix contains lists of lessons or warnings about pre-contract considerations and contract contents which emerged during the process described in Appendix 1. Though they lie slightly outside the main focus of this report (which is to concentrate on the management of the situation once outsourcing has been established), they are considered to be worth recording.

1.2 These lists are claimed to be practical rather than exhaustive – they arise from experience of outsourcing gained by managers of many companies and include items which, with the benefit of hindsight, managers wish they had taken into account. Many of these lessons learnt were extracted from the `any other comments' section of the Outsourcing Questionnaire responses.

Supplier selection & tender lessons

Evaluation/Negotiation

1   Avoid being committed to accepting the cheapest tender.

2   Establish tender marking strategy before tendering - stick to it.

3   Tender only those companies who meet the objective criteria.

4   Allow the supplier scope to negotiate and show innovation without compromising objectives.

5   Verify supplier claims by site visits and discussions with other customers.

6   Define expectations and assess the business understanding of suppliers when assessing tenders.

7   Request pre-tender information to check that potential suppliers can align with the objectives.

8   Verify the supplier organisation and that it can deliver the contracted service.

9   Verify the roles and responsibilities of transferred staff.

Supplier selection & tender lessons – continued

Communication/Understanding

10   At an early stage obtain Board commitment to outsourcing in principle.

11   Keep trade unions / staff associations informed throughout.

12   Clearly define outsourcing objectives - cost, flexibility, speed, expertise, innovation, reliability?

13   Ensure that the baseline in terms of service quality and costs is understood.

14   Do not hype up customer expectations beforehand, although some expectations are inevitable.

15   Keep customers informed throughout.

16   Between announcement and implementation, appraise line managers and IT staff of expectations.

17   Reassure users by explaining the contract and how it will be managed.

18   Ensure that end-users understand their obligations and potential business process changes.

19   Get the successful supplier to present to staff and selected customers as quickly as possible.

20   Ensure that requirements, deliverables and responsibilities are understood by all.

21   Keep procedures simple.

Management

22   Agree a schedule for completing the tendering exercise - stick to it.

23   Executives must recognise the impact and risks of outsourcing.

24   The Customer Contract Manager must have a good understanding of current services.

25   The Customer Contract Manager should be involved in supplier negotiation and selection.

26   Beware of supplier's under-achievement due to lack of business knowledge and resources.

27   Open book accounting should be an objective.

28   Identify the full cost of services before they are outsourced.

29   Outsource services which are well understood, not ill-defined problem areas.

30   Make renewal and termination subject to 12 months notice on either side.

31   The IS Department should retain responsibility for IS strategy.

32   The IS Department should retain accountability for the outsourced service.

Human Resource

33   If staff are to transfer, this is a vital part of contract negotiations.

34   The transfer of staff is key to future service quality – be willing to relinquish talented people.

35   Work with the supplier to keep transferred staff motivated.

36   Encourage continuing social contact with transferred staff.

37   Identify skills and the people who need to be retained – do not rely on chance.

Supplier selection & tender lessons – continued

Contract Content

38 You get what you pay for – and you only get what is in the contract.

39 Make sure the contract is sufficiently flexible to facilitate changes in business practice.

40 The prime contractor contract should cover everything within the scope of the outsourced work.

41 Take great care to avoid ambiguity about the scope and expectations of the contract.

42 Define formal change control mechanisms and include in the contract.

43 Define SLAs and include in the contract (as an appendix).

44 Define a charging scheme and include in the contract; make it flexible and easy to understand.

45 Define provision for contract re-negotiation and include in the contract.

46 Define penalties and include in the contract.

47 Include in the contract any verbal assurances received from the supplier.

48 Fully define problem escalation procedures for all parties.

49 Define disaster/contingency arrangements.

Appendix 3 Lessons Learnt – Best and Worst Consequences of Outsourcing

1.1 This Appendix contains lists of best and worst consequences of outsourcing as reported by over 100 organisations that responded to the Outsourcing Questionnaire prepared by the Outsourcing Working Group.

1.2 It is interesting to note that there are consequences of outsourcing which some organisations classify as `best consequences' whilst others classify them as `worst consequences'. No attempt has been made to expand or clarify the quotes or to investigate these apparent anomalies - the following lists contain literal quotes taken directly from the questionnaire responses.

Lessons learnt – Best consequence of outsourcing

Management Considerations

1 Reduces the range of IS activities and skill sets that need to be managed directly.

2 Concentrate on strategic issues, not mainframe operation.

3 Reduces bureaucracy.

4 Flexibility for future workload planning.

5 Enabled downsizing during a period of major business reorganisation.

6 Outsourcing enabled a move from highly centralised to decentralised systems.

7 Increased focus of management effort.

8 Enables the internal IT resource to focus time, resource and management on the value added services.

9 Reduced management effort.

10 Able to concentrate on systems definition, faster delivery and end-user service.

11 Outsourcing is used as an extension to the department.

Best consequences of outsourcing – continued

Customer Considerations

12   Become more customer oriented.

13   Need for stronger business ownership of systems.

14   Sharper focus and increased business understanding of the current contribution of IT.

Executive Considerations

15   More strategic view of IT.

HR Considerations

16   Bringing skills to the organisation with little or no start-up costs.

17   Less staff and better control of resources.

18   Little time is lost and number of staff are kept to a minimum.

19   IS staff (analysts become more aware of business issues and are able to expand their skills set).

20   Skills availability.

21   Greater expertise.

22   Expertise in all areas can be accessed in a cost-effective manner.

23   No need to hire/train highly skilled specialists.

24   Do not need to keep specialists in the company.

Service/Business Considerations

25   More flexible response to changing needs.

26   Improved mainframe operations.

27   Better quality services.

28   PC maintenance very effective and reasonably cheap.

29   Easier to plan and more likely to deliver on time.

30   Professional standards and expertise from the start.

31   Someone anticipating and taking care of problems before we notice them.

32   Systems developed sooner.

33   Delivery of bespoke developments on time and to budget.

34   Total control of software development.

35   Time for delivery of development work.

36   Commercial application packages.

37   Far easier for the network supplier to deal with changes.

38   Wide area network management.

39   Mainframe maintenance - expensive but high quality.

40   Better control of services.

Best consequences of outsourcing – continued

Communications/Understanding Considerations

41   Single point of ownership.

Financial Considerations

42   Predictable costs.

43   Effective cost control.

44   Reduction in IT costs.

45   Cost reduction by competition.

46   Reduced overheads.

47   Introduction of fixed price project development.

48   Conversion of fixed to variable costs.

49   Better control of maintenance and development costs.

50   Significant reduction in PC support costs.

51   Ability to flex costs very quickly.

52   Cost-effective support for geographically remote locations.

Lessons learnt – Worst consequences of outsourcing

Management Considerations

1 More management time spent dealing with disputed costs, estimates, scope of work etc.
2 Contract management falls on IS.
3 Extent of control needed.
4 Limited control of a supplier once a commitment has been made.
5 Loss of control and over-dependence.
6 Control of hardware contractors.
7 Lack of influence on the service provider.
8 Did not appreciate the strength of negotiation and account management skills required from the outset.
9 Areas of software support which involve a number of suppliers.
10 Getting the service right took 2 years.
11 Risk of lock-in to commercial contracts which lose relevance.
12 Complacency of supplier and buyer.
13 Lack of in-built site standards.
14 Preserving a status quo because it is out of sight.
15 Difficulty of reverting to in-house services.

Customer Considerations

16 Users do not like paying for external services.
17 Unrealistic expectations of users.
18 Ill-defined requirements.

Executive Considerations

19 Senior managers do not understand that experience of the business is essential and needs to be in-house.
20 Lack of integration with the corporate infrastructure.

HR Considerations

21 Not being in control of resources.
22 Loss of skills in the application of IT.
23 Fragmentation of IS capability - loss of internal learning.
24 Loss of professional IT competence within the organisation.
25 Staff unease, even though personnel issues have been high on the agenda of all outsourcing projects.
26 Uncertainty/destabilisation of staff.
27 Lack of business skills/knowledge.

Worst consequences of outsourcing – continued

Service/Business Considerations

28 Loss of flexibility.

29 Loss of responsiveness to the customer base.

30 Poor service levels – core systems downtime.

31 Slow reaction to change.

32 Slow reaction to critical problems.

33 Development projects – quality of delivered software very poor.

34 Poor project management, missed dates.

35 System performance problems on applications development.

36 Disastrous outsourcing of software development leaving in-house staff to pick up the pieces.

37 Less control of services.

38 Occasional difficulty in controlling contractors and getting the right level of service.

39 Dependence upon another organisation's procedures for service levels.

40 Reaction time sometimes not quick enough.

41 Occasional disasters.

42 Poor quality software maintenance.

43 PC maintenance – cheap and poor quality.

44 Finding a reliable maintenance provider for desk top hardware.

45 Total support of IT operations – a shambles.

46 Recovering if things go wrong.

47 Software support.

48 Exaggerated support claims.

49 Telecommunications.

Communications/Understanding Considerations

50 Danger of relinquishing responsibility.

51 Perception of `us' and `them'.

52 Understanding of business slow to transfer.

53 Areas where the contract has not been as precise and detailed as it should have been.

54 Poor contracts for development.

55 Systems applications with ill-defined requirements.

56 Lack of appreciation/understanding of the company's operations and needs.

57 Poor control by both parties and ambiguous accountability.

58 Taken a long time to establish a client relationship.

Worst consequences of outsourcing – continued

Financial Considerations

59 Price not reflecting cost reductions from changes in technology.

60 Costs relative to in-house costs.

61 A certain rigidity in the technical methodology in order to protect the income base, ie, lack of flexibility in responding to technical change.

62 Continue putting profits before our business benefits.

63 More expensive (although some in-house costs were hidden).

64 May be paying more than we should.

65 Cost over-runs for software development.

Appendix 4 Three Main Elements of Managing an Outsourcing Contract

Introduction

One of the guest presenters to the Outsourcing Working Group was Bob Aylott of Nolan Norton & Co. He discussed the relationships between Client Side/Contract Management, the Outsourcing Supplier and Users. Copies of six of the slides used by Bob in his presentation are contained in this appendix – the slides should be self explanatory.

Managing an Outsourcing Contract has Three Main Management Elements That Bind Together the Three Interested Parties

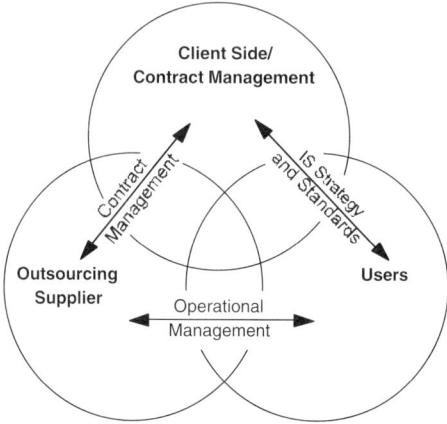

Contract Management is Concerned With

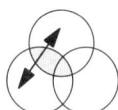

- Auditing supplier performance
- Implementing contract variations
- Dealing with charges and compensations
- Contracting for new services and projects

Operational Management is Concerned With

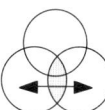

- Demanding and delivering services
- Resolving day to day operational problems
- Requesting and implementing routine change

IT Strategy and Standards is Concerned With

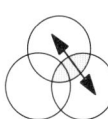

- Creating and maintaining the IS and IT Strategy
- Developing and implementing standards to support the strategy and the contract
- Developing IS/IT budgets for the organisation
- Auditing standards, strategy etc

Key Responsibilities

■ The user is responsible for exploiting the service to generate value

■ The Client Side is responsible for creating and maintaining the frameworks within which services are delivered and exploited - that is contracts, standards, strategies, budgets etc

■ The supplier is responsible for delivering the service demanded in accordance with the framework of contracts, standards etc

Additionally When There are Multiple Suppliers There is a Service Integration Role

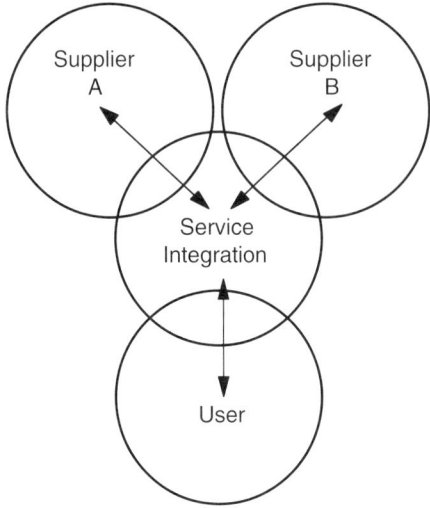

Appendix 5 Outsourcing Bibliography

Produced by IMPACT for the Outsourcing Working Group. Our thanks to Leslie Willcocks at Templeton College, Oxford for allowing us to include part of the bibliography from his forthcoming book (Last entry in the bibliography).

1   Ambrosio, J. `Outsourcing at Southland: Best of Times, Worst of Times'. Computerworld, Vol. 25, 12, March 25, 1991.

2   Apte, U.(1990) `Global Outsourcing of Information Systems and Processing Services'. The Information Society, Vol. 7, pp. 287-303.

3   Apte, U. & Maron, R.(1993). `Global Disaggregation of Information Services.' Paper presented at the Outsourcing of Information Systems Conference, University of Twente, The Netherlands, May 20-22, 1993.

4   Auwers, T. & Deschoolmeester, D.(1993) `The Dynamics of an Outsourcing Relationship: A Case in the Belgian Food Industry'. Paper presented at the Outsourcing of Information Systems Conference, University of Twente, The Netherlands, May 20-22, 1993.

5   Blair, D. `I Survived Outsourcing'. CIO, Vol. 3, 10 July 1990, pp. 20-24.

6   BCS (1993) `The Sourcer's Apprentice. A Guide to IT Outsourcing for Decision Makers'. BCS, Swindon.

7   Buck-Lew, M.(1992) `To Outsource or Not?' International Journal of Information Management, 12, pp. 3-20.

8   CCTA (1993) `Producing Contracts for Market Tested IS/IT Services'. ISBN 0 946683 71 9 HMSO, London.

9   CCTA (1993) `Evaluation of IS/IT Services'. ISBN 0 946683 69 7 HMSO, London.

10 CCTA (1993) `The Intelligent Customer'. ISBN 0 946683 64 6 HMSO, London.

11 CCTA (1993) `Market Testing IS/IT Provision'. ISBN 0 946683 63 8 HMSO, London.

12 CCTA (1993) `Defining IS/IT Services for Market Testing'. ISBN 0 946683 67 0 HMSO, London.

13 CCTA (1993) `The In-house Bid'. ISBN 0 946683 65 4 HMSO, London.

14 CCTA (1993) `Managing IS/IT for the Business'. The role of the Intelligent Customer ISBN 0 946683 74 3 Library CCTA, Norwich.

15 CCTA (1994) `Managing Contracts for IS/IT Services'. ISBN 0 11 3306601 HMSO, London.

16   Clark, T. & Zmud, R.(1993) `The Outsourcing Decision Structure: A Dynamic Modelling Approach'. Paper presented at the Outsourcing of Information Systems Conference, University of Twente, The Netherlands, May 20-22, 1993.

17   CSSA Briefing Note `An Introduction to Facilities Management'. Computing Services & Software Association, Hanover House, 73/74 High Holborn, London WC1V 6LE.

18   CSSA Briefing Note `In-house Computing or Facilities Management – the Real Costs'. Computer Services and Software Association, Hanover House, 73/74 High Holborn, London WC1V 6LE.

19   CSSA Code of Practice `Facilities Management'. Computer Services and Software Association, Hanover House, 73/74 High Holborn, London WC1V 6LE.

20   Drucker, P.(1991) `The Coming of the New Organisation'. In McGowan W (ed.) Revolution in Real Time. Harvard Business School Press, Boston.

21   Earl, M.(1991) `Outsourcing Information Services'. Public Money and Management, Autumn, pp. 17-21.

22   Feeny, D., Earl, M. & Edwards, B.(1989) `IS Arrangements to Suit Complex Organisations 2. Integrating the Effects of Users and Specialists'. OXIIM Research and Discussion Paper 89/5, Templeton College, Oxford.

23   Feeny, D., Willcocks, L., Rands, T. & Fitzgerald, G.(1993) `Strengths for IT Management - When Outsourcing Equals Rightsourcing'. In Rock, S. (ed.), Directors Guide to Outsourcing. Institute of Directors/IBM London.

24   Grant, R.(1992) `The Resource-based Theory of Competitive Advantage: Implications for Strategy Formulation'. Sloan Management Review. 33, 3 pp. 114-135.

25   Griese, J.(1993) `Outsourcing of Information Systems Services in Switzerland – A Status Report.' Paper presented at the Outsourcing of Information Systems Services Conference, University of Twente, The Netherlands, May 20-22, 1993.

26   Hammersmith, A. `Slaying the IS Dragon with Outsourcery'. Computerworld Vol. 23, 38, September 18, 1989, pp. 1-4.

27   Heinzl, A.(1993) `Outsourcing the Information Systems Function Within The Company – An Empirical Survey'. Paper presented at the Outsourcing of Information Systems Services Conference, University of Twente, The Netherlands, May 20-22, 1993.

28   Huber, R.(1993) `How Continental Bank Outsourced its Crown Jewels'. Harvard Business Review, January – February, pp. 121-129.

29   Huff, S. `Outsourcing of Information Services'. Business Quarterly, Vol. 55, 4, Spring, 1991, pp. 62-65.

30   International Data Corporation (1991) `The Impact of Facilities Management on the IT Market'. International Data Corporation, London.

31   Klepper, R. `Efficient Outsourcing Relationships.' Paper presented at the Outsourcing of Information Systems Services Conference, University of Twente, The Netherlands, May 20-22, 1993.

32   Krass, P. `The Dollars and Sense of Outsourcing'. Information Week Issue 259, February 26, 1990. pp. 26-31.

33 Lacity, M. & Hirschheim, R.(1992) `The Information Systems Outsourcing Bandwagon: Look before You Leap'. Paper presented at the OXIIM/PA Conference, Templeton College, Oxford (also in Sloan Management Review – September 1993).

34 Lacity, M. & Hirschheim, R.(1993) `Information Systems Outsourcing.' Wiley, Chichester.

35 Loh, L. & Venkatraman, N.(1992a) `Diffusion of Information Technology Outsourcing: Influence Sources and the Kodak Effect'. CISR Working Paper No. 245, October, Massachusetts Institute of Technology, Cambridge, USA.

36 Loh, L. & Venkatraman, N.(1992b) `Determinants of Information Technology Outsourcing: A Cross Sectional Analysis'. Journal of Management Information Systems, 9,1, pp. 7-24.

37 Loh, L. & Venkatraman, N.(1992) `Stock Market Reactions to Information Technology Outsourcing: An Event Study'. Working Paper No. 3499-92 BPS, Massachusetts Institute of Technology, Cambridge, USA.

38 Moad, J.(1993) `Inside an Outsourcing Deal'. Datamation, 15th February, pp. 20-27.

39 Morgan, W. and Gladyszewski, S. `Outsourcing: The Great Debate'. Computerworld, Vol. 23, 50, December 11, 1989, pp. 69-74.

40 O'Leary, M. `The Mainframe Doesn't Work Here Anymore'. CIO, Vol. 6, 6, June 1990, pp. 27-35.

41 Oltman, J. `21st Century Outsourcing'. Computerworld, Vol. 24, 16, April 16, 1990, pp. 77-79.

42 Prahalad, C. & Hamel, G.(1991) `The Core Competence of the Corporation'. Harvard Business Review, 63, 3, pp. 79-91.

43 Quinn, J.(1992) `The Intelligent Enterprise: A New Paradigm'. Academy of Management Executive, 6, 4, pp. 44-63.

44 Quinn, J., Doorley, T. & Paquette, P.(1990) `Technology in Services: Rethinking Strategic Focus'. Sloan Management Review, 31, 2, pp. 79-87.

45 Rands, T.(1991) `A Framework for Management Software Make/Buy'. Management Research Paper 91/8, Templeton College, Oxford.

46 Saaksjarvi, M.(1993) `Outsourcing of Information Systems: Matching Organisational Forms and Organisational Roles'. Paper presented at the Outsourcing of Information Systems Services Conference, University of Twente, The Netherlands, May 20-22, 1993.

47 Scott Morton, M. (1989) `Management and IT in the Nineties'. In Innovation Through Information Technology: Managing Change. Amdahl Executive Institute, London.

48 Symons, C.(1993) `Analysing the Strategic Impact of Outsourcing on Your Company's Competitive Position'. Internal Working Paper, Nolan Norton, London.

49 Willcocks, L.(1994) `Managing Information Systems in UK Public Administration: Issues and Prospects'. Public Administration, March, 1994.

50 Willcocks, L. and Fitzgerald, G.(1993) `IT Outsourcing: Preliminary Findings from Recent UK Research'. OXIIM RDP 93/10 Oxford.

51   Willcocks, L. and Fitzgerald, G.(1994) `*Successful Outsourcing – When and how to put your IT out of house'*. London: Business Intelligence.

Appendix 6 Acknowledgements

The following organisations have been represented at Working Group meetings:

Army*
Bank of England*
BAA*
CCTA*
Employment Department
Longman*
Nuclear Electric
Office of Population Censuses and Surveys (OPCS)
Rhône Poulenc
TSB Bank
ABB Transportation
Granada UK Rental
Nolan Norton & Co
SHL Systemhouse
IMPACT*

* These organisations were also represented in Outsourcing Sub Groups.

The Working Group gratefully acknowledges the value of the contribution of over 100 companies that completed the Outsourcing questionnaire.

Appreciation is also expressed to Vaughn Hovey, Manager, IT Supplier and Alliance Management for Eastman Kodak Company, who took time to comment on a late draft of the report when he visited the UK in March 1995 to present at the IMPACT Distinguished Seminar "Can Outsourcing Really be a Partnership?"

IMPACT OUTSOURCING GUIDELINES
Management Issues

1 | Retain in-house control over strategic direction.
2 | Retain responsibility for setting standards to which the supplier must conform.
3 | Use a prime contractor.
4 | Make the supplier responsible for delivery.
5 | Be prescriptive about the service requirements rather than the method of service delivery.
6 | Never lose sight of the business driven objectives of outsourcing.
7 | Avoid lock-in to a single supplier.
8 | Accept value for money but accept the supplier's need to make a profit – a partnership.
9 | Understand the strategic, political and managerial implications of the scope of your outsourcing.
10 | Define supplier's points of contact – ensure adherence.
11 | Having an appropriate person to manage the contract is key (see Section 4).
12 | Keep the procedures simple.
13 | Regularly review the outsourcing contract and relationship with the supplier.
14 | Never stop negotiating.
15 | Re-tender contracts at defined intervals.
16 | Regularly review the outsourcing market to identify trends and changes.
17 | Monitor supplier's resource levels and business knowledge.
18 | Encourage co-operative contract evolution to take advantage of developing technologies.
19 | Retain and exercise the right to conduct IS audits at supplier's premises.
20 | Aim for continuous improvement.

Human Resource Issues

21 | Ensure sufficient number and quality of in-house staff remain to manage the outsourced situation (see Section 4).
22 | Promote a continuing bond between supplier staff and end-users.
23 | Make the morale of supplier staff a customer concern.
24 | Sort out personality conflicts as soon as possible.
25 | Review regularly in-house staff skills and numbers.
26 | Involve end-users in monitoring service delivery against targets (see Section 6).
27 | Retain the right to veto supplier's choice of key staff.

Service/Business Issues

28 | Match expectations with needs, not historical achievments.
29 | Have a contingency escape plan covering the outsourcing contract, software ownership etc.
30 | Maintain the right to invite tenders for new work.
31 | Recognise that requirements will change and be willing to adjust costs accordingly.
32 | Ensure that SLAs are always realistic and do not expect them to remain static (see Section 5).
33 | Continue to benchmark the service and consider alternative approaches.
34 | Discuss with all concerned, at the earliest possible stage, plans which could affect services.

Communication/Understanding Issues

35 | Clearly define the scope and interfaces of what is outsourced.
36 | Establish unambiguous roles and responsibilities for the customer, end-users and supplier (see Appendix 4).
37 | Maintain regular customer/supplier contact at various levels – even when things are going well.
38 | Establish an open relationship – be prepared to compromise.
39 | Build a relationship of trust with supplier.
40 | Hold regular meetings to monitor achievements (see Section 6).
41 | Define clear escalation procedures.
42 | Do not abuse escalation procedures – nit picking with managers is counter productive.
43 | Encourage the supplier to propose changes based on their expertise.
44 | Ensure customer awareness, understanding and commitment.

Printed in the UK for HMSO Dd 301435 C10 10/95 9385 3240